STARTING WITH
BUDGERIGARS

Kurt Kolar

Translated by Astrid Mick
Edited by David Alderton

BLANDFORD

Contents

Introduction

Of all domestic birds, none is as popular or as widely kept as the budgerigar. This parakeet does indeed possess many advantages as a pet. It may live for as long as 15 years, it is not expensive to care for, it is easy for friends or other family members to look after it while you are on holiday, it does not make a lot of noise and it will even seek close contact with its human carers. Nevertheless it is not a good idea to take on a budgerigar without giving the matter some thought beforehand.

Perhaps you are already a budgerigar-owner and just want to know more about looking after them, or you may be a beginner. In both cases, you should be keen on looking after your pet properly and should be very aware of the responsibility involved. This will also involve certain expenses that will end up being more than the initial outlay for the bird.

The most important commitment is to keep the bird in a manner appropriate to its species. What does this mean? Even experts on animal care often disagree on this aspect. We need to know how these creatures live in their natural habitat and this does not just mean knowing the appropriate food. Do they fly about a great deal in the wild? Do they like to climb or do they prefer to be on the ground? Do they require a hiding place? Are they solitary animals or do they prefer a social life? There are references to the lifestyles of budgerigars in the wild and in the home throughout this book.

Keeping pets will only work in the long run if all family members are agreeable to the idea. Only then will everybody feel comfortable and that, of course, will ultimately include your budgerigar.

A budgerigar as a present?

Many people love giving and receiving pets as presents. In principle, there is nothing wrong with trying to give someone pleasure with a present of an animal but, when giving a budgerigar certain important preconditions need to be met. You should find out for certain whether the recipient really will enjoy keeping a bird and is in a position, and willing, to take on all the duties connected with its keeping and care, without it becoming a burden.

For example, if you make a present of a budgerigar to someone who spends a great deal of time travelling, or who is allergic to the fine dust inevitably generated when keeping birds – although, luckily, this is fairly rare – the pet may easily become a problem.

Other points which need to be considered are discussed in the following pages. You will then be able to make your own decision, based primarily on the consideration that both the owner and the pet should be equally fulfilled.

Where to keep your budgerigar

Correct and regular care is a basic prerequisite for the well-being of any pet, and birds, more than many other creatures, require good, clean air. If there is a heavy smoker in the family, you should avoid keeping budgerigars or other birds. Neither should a bird be kept in the kitchen. This can be extremely dangerous – if non-stick cooking utensils overheat, the fumes will be deadly.

Dry air in a room will not harm budgerigars because they originate from regions where the humidity is low. They will also be all right in an unheated room. Temperatures of 10°C (50°F) and below will not upset a budgerigar at all. Of course, a budgerigar that is kept at a temperature of 20°C (68°F) for most of the time – a room temperature that is pleasant for people – should not be subjected to sudden drops in temperature.

Dirt or unpleasant smells are seldom a problem when keeping budgerigars, but tiny feathers and seed husks tend to get wafted out of the cage as the birds fly about, especially if there is no cover around the base of the cage. This is not a great problem, particularly if you have a vacuum-cleaner, but many people do not relish the prospect of the mess. The obsessively houseproud would be better off without pets.

The right kind of cage

Do not allow yourself to be too impressed by the colour and shape of a cage. The most important consideration should be its

For most budgerigars, their owner's living-room is their main home for their entire lives. There are many ways of helping a small bird feel at ease here.

Cages, whatever their size, should be positioned in a bright corner or at least on a wall, never in the middle of a room! Protection from draughts is essential.

5

suitability for the pet and also for the owner. The size will depend largely on whether your bird is to remain in its cage for most of the time or be able to fly freely around the room every day. f the latter applies, 50 cm (20 in) is the **minimum length** of cage that can be recommended. As far as width is concerned, the bird should be able to stretch its wings freely (this is a legal requirement in some countries). This will be sufficient for sleeping and temporary visits. Even budgerigars living in the wild will spend hours every day resting in one place.

Birdcages can be purchased with **vertical** or **horizontal bars**. A model with horizontal bars on at least two sides of the cage will be adequate for your pet. Budgerigars love climbing, and are very expert at it, so they will be able to exercise on the sides of the cage and thus utilize it to the full. Rectangular rather than circular cages are best for birds and they are generally easier to clean.

Finally, there is a choice between a cage with chrome-coated bars and one with plastic-coated bars. Provided that bird-mess stuck to the bars is removed fairly quickly, metal bars will remain good-looking for a long time but, inevitably, rust will start to appear, often in the corners first. Cages with an epoxy coating can be obtained in a range of different colours. These are simpler to clean and their attractive appearance can be maintained easily, provided that the coating remains intact.

Hen budgerigars in particular may use their strong bills to gnaw at the plastic-coated bars as well as at the perches. This may result in the dark-coloured wire becoming visible under the layer of coloured plastic. Eventually the wire will rust where it is exposed, particularly if it becomes wet.

With their strong bills, budgerigars are also capable of breaking the little plastic clips that secure the food-containers to the walls in some cages. This problem can be avoided by choosing a cage with metal fixtures.

Some cages are equipped with only a simple tray for a floor. These cages are cheap, and are often bought for this reason, but they can be difficult to clean thoroughly if they cannot be dismantled. In cages with a detachable base, the part of the cage with bars has to be lifted off for cleaning, thus providing your budgerigar with an excellent opportunity for escaping into the

A huge range of different types of cages awaits the buyer in pet-stores.

A simply shaped cage with vertical walls is the most suitable. The floor section should have a tray that can be pulled out.

room. Always check beforehand that your pet will be safe in the room, closing all windows and doors and excluding other pets, such as cats.

A ladder presents ample opportunity for climbing.

Equipping the cage

Many cage-manufacturers call their products 'bird-homes' but more often than not these so-called 'homes' are inadequately equipped. The **perches** or **ladders** are often unsuitable, and are seldom of the right diameter for the bird's feet to get a good grip and thus to ensure that their claws are worn down naturally. Usually the perches are far too thin. The plastic perches supplied with many cages are easy to clean but, because of their smooth surface, the claws are not worn down and grow too long. Also budgerigars cannot gnaw these perches as they would gnaw branches in the wild.

If the cage is large enough, you should replace these plastic

7

A food-container with a cover.

An automatic feeder is easy to check.

Drinking-water dispensers can be fixed to the bars of the cage.

perches with a few **branches**. These should be of sufficient diameter to allow your budgerigar to rest comfortably, with its hind toes not coming into contact with its front toes. You can cut branches from various fruit trees, as well as from willow, beech, poplar, alder, birch, maple or elder, and your birds will like to gnaw at these. Avoid any branches that have been recently sprayed and be sure to wash them before use, in case they have been soiled by wild birds.

When installing these perches, make sure that there are no other perches, ladders, toys or open food-containers immediately below them, as otherwise these are likely to become fouled with the birds' droppings.

Automatic feeders are very good and the seeds in them will nearly always remain clean. However, depending on the design, they may sometimes become blocked, so always check twice daily that the seeds are flowing freely. Automatic **drinking-water dispensers** are also excellent. Sick birds, which spend most of their time on the floor, need to be able to find water and food at this level.

Many birds get much enjoyment from splashing about in a **bird-bath**, which can be fixed around the cage-door.

Finally, the floor should be covered with a thin layer of **sand**. This not only helps to bind the droppings but is also a useful digestive aid for all seed-eating birds (see p. 21). Of all types of sand on sale in pet-stores, washed river sand is the most highly recommended. **Sandsheets** are another option, although they are often shredded by the budgerigars, especially by hens as they come into breeding condition.

Choosing a budgerigar

One budgerigar or several?

Budgerigars are naturally sociable and are never encountered as solitary birds in their natural habitat. After they have left their immediate family group, the young birds live in larger flocks for a few months. After that, they will find a partner, forming a bond that can last a lifetime, although they do tend to be fickle with their partners. Outside of breeding times, budgerigars are often found in huge flocks at feeding or watering sites, or in roosting trees.

Any owner who has watched closely how much time the individuals of a pair spend in preening each other's plumage and in other affectionate activities, such as mutual feeding, will have to admit that he or she could never spend that much time on a pet budgerigar.

A barely mature budgerigar kept as a solitary bird will soon form a close bond not only with its carer but also with various objects that it finds to play with in its cage. Cock birds will perform courtship displays to a human ear, nose or finger as they grow older. They will do the same with dummy budgerigars and other plastic figures, which they sometimes treat as a partner and, on other occasions, as a rival.

Any pet-lover with a little insight will think seriously about keeping such a sociable little bird as a solitary pet. You may decide instead to choose a pair of budgerigars, particularly if you have to go out to work during the day. They will then keep each other company.

This is how the claws grip a perch. Left: *While awake.* Right: *While sleeping.*

A cock bird or a hen?

If you lay great store by tame birds, you should start by keeping only one bird in your home and then, after 2–3 weeks, introduce the second one. If you spend a lot of time with it, a young budgerigar will become very tame within those few weeks. Thus, when the second young bird is introduced, it will have a model to copy and may well become finger-tame with its owner even sooner.

As your birds mature, you can restrict their breeding activities if required. In fact, successful breeding seldom occurs if no nesting box is provided! In addition budgerigars often only mate success-

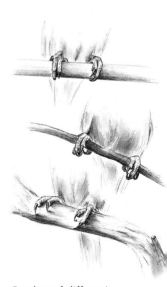

Perches of different thickness; the middle perch is completely unsuitable.

9

fully if they are part of a larger group of birds. Nevertheless, if you wish to eliminate any chance of breeding, it is a good idea to keep two cock birds. These will get on quite well together and are generally less of a problem than two hens, which are likely to be more quarrelsome.

A young budgerigar or an older one?

Should you intend to start breeding budgerigars, then you would do better to acquire mature birds about 1 year old. If you prefer to have tame birds, look for very young budgerigars about 6–8 weeks old.

Serious retailers or breeders will certainly advise you on your choice of budgerigar but it is still reassuring to know how to distinguish older from younger birds, and cocks from hens. A budgerigar's powers of mimicry are not related to its colour.

There is always a great demand for 'nestling' budgerigars but young birds that are still spending time in the nest are still not able to feed themselves entirely on their own. Not until about a week or two after flying from the nest – when they are about 6 weeks old – will they be independent of their parents and fit to be passed on to a new owner. People are often surprised by the appearance of young budgerigars, expecting them to be a tiny scrap rather than a bird which, apart from its much shorter tail, looks very much like an adult.

The following features characterize a budgerigar chick that has just left its nest:

Viewed close up, you can clearly see the long lashes around the eyes.

- **Dark irises** dominate the large eyes, which are usually black or red, depending on the colour variety of the bird.
- **Wavy markings** on the head look slightly washed out and unclear, and extend right down over the forehead, although this area is free of barring in an adult bird. The rest of the plumage is slightly duller in colour than that of a mature budgerigar.
- The **bill** is almost black, particularly towards the tip and especially in the case of grey and other relatively dark-coloured birds. The black colouring will disappear once the chick has been out of the nest for a short while.
- The **cere** – the featherless area between the upper bill and forehead – is pinkish to pale lilac in cocks while in hens it is often slightly paler and less prominent, with the area around the nostrils being whitish.

These differences in colour are not always well defined, however, so mistakes in **sexing** young birds are, therefore, quite likely on occasions. It is much easier to sex birds when they have acquired their adult colouring. In green and blue adult males the cere is blue,

whereas, in cock birds of other colour varieties, notably albino (pure white), lutino (pure yellow) and some pied birds, it is the same colour as in the young. All mature hens have a brown cere above the bill, which darkens in colour as they approach breeding condition.

Breeders will often also have the slightly larger, more expensive show budgerigars for sale. These should be treated in the same way as ordinary, pet-type budgerigars.

How to recognize a healthy budgerigar

Once you have selected a bird for its sex and colouring, you will also want to know whether it is really healthy. Here are a few points that will allow the beginner to make a reasonably sound judgement.

Make a preliminary check by standing sufficiently far away from the cage for the birds to continue to act in a normal fashion. You can recognize a sick budgerigar by the way it tightens up its plumage. Its eyes will not be open properly, its feathers will be fluffed up and it will be sleepier than usual. There may be other signs as well, such as green droppings on the floor of the cage.

You should choose a budgerigar that appears alert and lively. Once the retailer or breeder has taken it out of its cage you can carry out further checks:

Attention! A cardboard box will not last for very long under the onslaught of a budgerigar's bill.

- Be sure that it is **well nourished.** You should be able to feel the breast muscle on either side of the breastbone along the midline of the bird's underside. A distinct hollow here indicates weight loss.
- There should be **no secretions** from the eyes or bill.
- The area around the **vent** should be clean.
- Take a good look at the areas around the eyes and bill. If you see any whitish encrustations this is an indication of infestation with **scaly-face mites.**
- Check the bird's **legs** because, occasionally, a claw may be missing – or even an entire toe. This would not be a great calamity, merely a blemish, although in a show budgerigar this would ruin its exhibition potential.
- Check that the budgerigar can **fly** properly and has tail feathers of the right length. It could otherwise be affected by the feather disease called 'French moult'.
- If the bird is wearing a **leg-ring**, take the opportunity to check the year engraved on the ring; this should correspond to the bird's date of hatching. This is particularly important when buying, birds such as the lutino cock, as the colour of the cere remains the same throughout the bird's life (see p 10). The year will be entered in an abbreviated form, e.g. '97' for 1997, often alongside the individual's ring number and the breeder's initials.

12

Transporting your budgerigar home safely

A convincing picture of friendship: synchronized movements as if on command.

Often a buyer will ask the retailer to place the bird directly in its cage for the journey home. This is usually because he or she is worried that the bird might escape at home while being transferred to its cage.

This is not to be recommended, however, as there is a real risk of the bird getting nervous and excited in the strange cage and breaking off feathers on the bars or even injuring itself. Only birds that have had a long time to adjust to their environment should be transported in their own cage – and even then they may still be frightened on occasions!

It is far less risky to transport the bird in a small box, obtainable from a pet-store, or, for a short period, to put it in a secure, collapsible, cardboard box with small ventilation holes punched around the sides. Only one bird at a time should be transported in these small boxes.

When moving a sick bird, e.g. to a veterinarian, you need to take particular care:
- Never try to catch a bird in hot, muggy weather in the summer or carry it in your hand. This applies especially to overweight

13

birds. Put it in a box first, that has plenty of ventilation and never put it in your pocket! Walk in the shade.

- In a car, make sure that the box or carton is not in the sun. Never leave the bird in a locked car as this is likely to prove fatal if it is hot, even within a few minutes. Put the bird behind the front seat, on the floor, and never in the boot (trunk), as lethal exhaust fumes could leak into this compartment.
- In winter, hold the box under your jacket or wrap it in paper or a cloth. Avoid travelling long distances. In extremely cold weather, heat up the car first.

Adjustment period

It is desirable to have the cage prepared before your bird arrives. Then you will need only to add food and water. The best idea is to sprinkle a little food on the floor of the cage for the first few days and hang up some spray millet close to a perch in order to persuade the budgerigar to eat in its new surroundings. You can then place the budgerigar in its new home.

Remember that your budgerigar has just been separated from

14

its companions and kept in a small carrying box possibly for an hour or more. Suddenly, it finds itself in yet another new situation and this will be stressful. It is best to leave it alone for a while.

Even if the new arrival refuses to leave its carrying box immediately, do not get impatient. Your budgerigar should be given a chance to take its time looking around and jumping out into the cage. Do not allow all the curious members of your family to form a circle around the cage and frighten the little bird even more.

For a few days, the budgerigar will probably sit around quietly because it is unaccustomed to being separated from its companions so suddenly. If you have brought two birds home with you, they should soon regain their usual cheerfulness more quickly.

Once the newcomer has settled down, which may take various lengths of time, depending on the individual bird, you may make the first attempts at taming it. If you are happy enough just to observe your birds, you need do no more at this point. You can provide them with what they need but otherwise leave them in peace.

Taming your budgerigar

Those of you who are keen to handle your bird from the start, should try to win the trust of your new pet. The bird needs to lose its fear of the human hand as its past experiences have probably not been very encouraging.

Sometimes budgerigar-owners are advised to cut off the tips of some of their bird's flight feathers so that it can be allowed out of its cage with less risk of injuring itself. Please forget about this. In any case, it is not really something that you should undertake yourself. Ask your veterinarian for advice because, if the feathers are cut at too early a stage, severe bleeding may result.

Any bird-lover should know all about the food requirements of his or her birds and be familiar with the different types of food.

The best means of training your new pet will involve food. Proffer something that your budgerigar likes to eat, e.g. a piece of spray millet or chickweed (*Stellaria media*). It will soon become interested but will probably not be brave enough to take this delicacy from your hand. Be patient and hold out a piece of food like this to it every day and it will soon climb onto your hand. To begin with your budgerigar will be very hesitant but it will soon think nothing of jumping straight onto your hand. This is the time when you can also start to allow it to fly around in the room.

The right foods for your budgerigar

In their native Australian habitat, budgerigars' staple diet consists of various grass seeds in different stages of ripeness. Even more

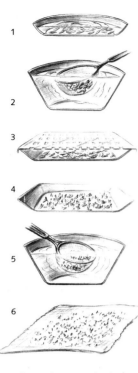

than the hard, dry seeds that form their regular diet, they love the softer, green ones, with their milky, half-ripe grains. These can be offered regularly if they are available but first be sure that the plants have not been sprayed with any herbicides.

Standard seed mixtures

The seed mixtures sold for budgerigars consist mainly of grass seeds, notably various millets. The largest proportion of seed mixtures usually consists of either yellow **Plata millet** or white **pearl millet** – a slightly larger seed. Also in the mixture, although less popular with the budgerigars themselves, are the red seeds of **Dakota millet.**

The somewhat elongated, shiny brownish grains are known as 'canary seed'. There may also be some dehulled oats, also called 'groats', although these tend to be relatively fattening. Some seed mixtures today are supplemented with vitamins and minerals, which help to compensate for deficiencies in the seeds.

Specially formulated **dry foods**, which can be used in place of seed mixtures, are also available, if your bird will eat them. You can also augment your budgerigar's diet by providing some **softfood** in a separate container. This will provide extra protein and other essential nutrients. The contents of this container should be renewed every day.

As long as there are no titbits or millet sprays to entice it, your budgerigar will be quite happy eating just the seed mixture on its own, although variety is important in a budgerigar's diet. It will pick grain after grain out of the seed-pot, crack the husks and discard them.

As the husks usually fall straight back into the seed-pot, they tend to form a layer on the top and the budgerigar is unlikely to attempt to get at the seeds beneath. At a brief glance there may seem to be enough food left. It would be a waste of food to pour away the entire contents of the seed-pot, so just gently blow off the empty husks over a dustbin each day and top up the pot as necessary.

Preparing germinated seeds

You can improve the nutritional value of dry seeds, raising both the protein and Vitamin B levels at the same time, by offering your birds seeds that have been germinated (see left).

The only disadvantage is that germinated seeds will not keep long. In warm weather they will go rancid after a few hours and will then be potentially dangerous to the birds. The pots used should be cleaned out every day, as with softfood.

Preparing germinated seeds:
1. *Place the required daily quantity in a flat dish. Pour in enough water to just cover the seeds.*
2. *After 24 hours in a warm position the seeds will swell up.*
3. *Rinse the seeds well in a sieve and then spread them out flat in a dish. Cover them to prevent them from drying out.*
4. *The first shoots will appear during the next 24 hours.*
5 & 6. *After rinsing and drying on absorbent paper, this delicacy will be ready to serve. Do not allow the shoots to turn mouldy – this will be dangerous for your pet.*

Previous page: *All budgerigars enjoy a spray of millet.*

Opposite above: *Fresh lettuce leaves also form part of a regular supply of greenfood and are much enjoyed.*

Opposite below: *Pinecones filled with seeds provide a welcome activity for little bills.*

Spray millet and other delicacies

Our budgerigars, love picking grains off natural seedheads. Spray **millets** are much more popular than the seeds offered in a food-container.

Sick birds that will take hardly any notice of normal food can often be encouraged to eat if offered their favourite spray millet. The seeds still attached to the seedhead are not quite as dry and appear to be much easier to digest than the usual food.

A wide range of other delicacies can be found in pet-stores, in the form of, e.g., **crackers**, **bells** or **hearts.** The base is generally the usual seed mixture with added vitamins, made into different shapes with a binding substance. Avoid coloured treats if possible as these are likely to colour your pet's droppings, which could be mistaken for enteritis. Budgerigars love to nibble at these shapes and they provide an extra focus of interest, helping to prevent boredom

Supplements

A range of food mixtures with special additives is also available. These can all be given at any time and they will provide a valuable variety to the diet. **Iodine**, **honey** and **cod-liver-oil capsules** – obtainable in small pouches – are often used as supplements to normal food. You can also buy supplements, in both powder and liquid form, intended specifically for birds. Read the instructions carefully because overdosing can be harmful, and even fatal.

Greenfood and vitamins

You can grow millet in the spring after the last frosts, using budgerigar seed mixture. By late summer the green seedheads start to ripen and turn brown, providing a delicacy not only for budgerigars but for all seed-eating birds.

In addition to seed, greenfood should be a regular item on the menu. Budgerigars love **chickweed** (*Stellaria media*), or offer a clean **lettuce** leaf – all free of pesticides, of course! The germinating kits that are on sale will provide birds with fresh greenfood as well. You may also offer budgerigars a piece of apple or carrot. Greenfood helps to provide essential vitamins which are lacking in the budgerigar's seed diet.

Water for drinking or bathing

In their native Australia, budgerigars live in areas where there is often no rain for months. They have to undertake flights over long

Budgerigars do not drink a lot and their enjoyment of a bath will depend a lot on the individual bird. A bird-bath should be available, however, just in case. It can be hung on the outside of the cage in front of one of the doors.

A delightful activity: two budgerigars grooming each other's plumage and nibbling at each other's bills – their first attempts at mutual feeding.

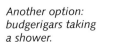

Another option: budgerigars taking a shower.

distances to find water as well as food. After long periods of thirst they will plunge right into the shallow water at the edge of a pond or lake. Budgerigars are able to survive longer than most birds without drinking any water.

As they are very frugal in this respect, budgerigars in cages may well only rarely be seen drinking water. Nevertheless, they should always be supplied with pure, clean water and they will drink every day. Breeding pairs will often consume quite large volumes of water when they have chicks in the nest. If drinking-quality water is not available from your mains tap, your birds can be given still mineral water, although again this must be changed daily.

The water in their bird-bath should also be suitable for drinking purposes because budgerigars are unable to distinguish between drinking and bathing water.

Not all budgerigars will delight their owners and fulfil their expectations by happily splashing about in a bird-bath, which can be fixed around the door of their cage, thus preventing water from being splashed over the adjacent furniture. Some budgerigars prefer to bathe in a flat dish or to slide around between wet leaves. Others will have nothing to do with water or prefer a shower.

They will sit beside a dripping tap and allow themselves to be splashed or misted with a plant-sprayer. If your birds do like to

20

bathe, they should be given opportunities to do so all year round, not just in hot summer weather. Bathing helps to prevent feather dust accumulating outside the cage.

Calcium, grit and charcoal

Minerals are also essential for budgerigars, with calcium and phosphorus being particularly important.

Some budgerigars derive great enjoyment from demolishing a **cuttlefish bone**. In this case, take heart in the thought that this is a good pastime for exercising and filing down their bills. There are special clips for attaching cuttlefish bones to the cage bars and holding them in place. Position the bone close to a perch so that your budgerigar can reach it easily.

Particles of grit act like tiny millstones in the crops of seed-eating birds. They help to grind down seeds, assisting the digestive process.

Not every type of grit is suitable for the purpose. River sand or beach sand is best as it contains no sharp-edged particles that might harm the birds. So-called 'shell sand' has a high chalk content which dissolves in the stomach and is not good for the bird in large quantities.

Some grits contain small amounts of charcoal. This home remedy has been used to counteract the effects of diarrhoea and other digestive upsets and will also help budgerigars in such cases.

Cuttlefish bone (top) *or a piece of limestone* (bottom) *can be fixed to a holder on the side of the cage.*

21

Does your budgerigar need playthings?

The most important thing for a budgerigar is a companion. The partners will stimulate each other to engage in activities and the pair may spend an hour or more a day in mutual grooming of feathers alone.

In the wild, feeding sites and watering places may be very far apart and travelling between them can take a considerable time. From early in the morning until late at night budgerigars have to be constantly alert, watching out for birds of prey or snakes that might represent a threat to them.

Captive budgerigars miss all this and you may imagine that they live a more carefree life under these circumstances. Certainly they have much more 'leisure time' as domestic pets and this means that we must make sure that they are kept occupied.

Branches for climbing purposes can be difficult to fit in a small cage, so it is a good idea to have a small forked tree-branch in a corner of the room which the birds can use when they are allowed out of their cage.

A many-forked branch of a fruit tree, a sycamore tree or elder,

Without the challenges of life in the wild, budgerigars in captivity, especially those without a partner, may become bored. The answer is to provide them with plenty of playthings, a means of exercise and to spend time with them.

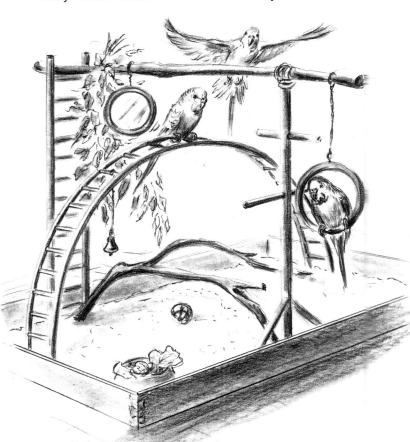

A playground like this offers plenty of variety for a budgerigar. If desired, the whole unit can be rearranged at any time.

secured in a large flowerpot or Christmas-tree stand, will soon become their favourite place to spend time. Budgerigar 'playgrounds' can also be purchased which provide the birds with rungs, ladders and a swing, and plenty of variety. A swing in the cage will provide a budgerigar with a means of exercise as it will have to make the appropriate muscular adjustments when landing onto a swing. The most fortunate budgerigars, however, are those whose owners have given them a partner.

Budgerigars come in a wide range of colours apart from the natural light green form.

Solitary birds will need to be kept occupied by their owner and be given attention for much of the time. This can be accomplished by spending a little extra effort when feeding them (see p. 18), by giving them an opportunity to gnaw and nibble at different things, and by putting different objects in their cage for them to experience. These do have to not be any of the popular plastic playdolls; often a small pebble, table-tennis ball or a little bell will be sufficient.

Personally, I prefer to see a budgerigar doing acrobatics on a natural branch than on a garish yellow plastic ladder and seeing it playing affectionately with its partner rather than trying in vain to establish contact with its own reflection in a mirror. Take care when choosing ladders for young budgerigars to use. An immature bird may get trapped between the rungs of the ladder if they are not properly spaced.

Regular tasks

All activities in which budgerigars engage are accompanied by vocalizations – something that not everyone will be thrilled about, especially in the summer when it gets light very early. They can be controlled to some extent by covering up the cage with a dark cloth at night. Avoid using a loosely woven fabric in which your bird's claws could become caught. As soon as you remove the cloth in the morning, your budgerigar will be 'switched on' and will embark cheerfully on its daily activities.

Tame birds will often follow the daily rhythm of their owners and remain quiet until they get up. Whatever the case may be, you should make sure that the budgerigars enjoy the same length of peace each night after 12 hours of being awake. If the cage is in the living-room, where the television may be producing flickering coloured light until late, you should cover up the cage. Excessive exposure to light may interfere with the budgerigar's natural rhythms and result in, e.g., abnormal moulting patterns. Voices and music at normal levels will not disturb the birds so much.

The importance of cleanliness

The most important rule when keeping any kind of animal is cleanliness. In particular, all food- and water-containers must be kept scrupulously clean and will therefore need to be washed regularly. Water-containers get dirty quickest of all and dirt tends to collect in the corners. Tubular drinking-vessels, and their spouts, can be cleaned with a bottle-brush. Provided that the food-container has not been polluted with droppings it will be sufficient to blow the empty seed husks off the top. You will need to add only a small portion of seeds. If the perches are soiled with droppings they should be removed straight away and either replaced or scrubbed thoroughly. Any dirt clinging to the bars of the cage should also be removed so that the chrome or brass coating of the bars does not discolour as a result of chemical reactions. A cloth and warm water should be adequate for this purpose.

On the floor tray the area under the perches will become most heavily soiled. You may have to remove the droppings with a trowel or a scraper if you are covering the floor with bird-sand, although sandsheets can just be replaced.

Droppings should never be left to lie around for a long time as they will dry up rapidly and the dust may then be whirled up and spread about by the bird's wingbeats. It can then be inhaled by both birds and people – not good for anyone's health.

Even in the wild, the daily rhythm of budgerigars is strictly regulated, with the advent of dawn and dusk being particularly important. After stretching their wings in the morning and grooming their plumage, the next item on the programme will be a meal.

A much-loved delicacy: a heart made of seeds that gives budgerigars plenty to do.

Weekly routine

A general cleaning out at least once a week should be part of the regular routine. The food-containers – even if there is no visible dirt – and the entire cage should all be washed thoroughly.

While the budgerigars are flying around in the room, take the part of the cage with bars outdoors and wipe down the sides carefully. If the birds are to remain in their cage, the plastic tray at least should be thoroughly cleaned. Birds that fly around freely in a room will soil the areas beneath their regular perching places. Sheets of newspaper laid down in these areas will make cleaning easier.

Conscientious owners should not forget that budgerigars are generally not very happy about cleaning activities in the room and brooms being brandished will create a flight reaction and considerable stress to the bird.

A vacuum-cleaner with its loud whirring noise may be frightening so, for this reason, be careful when using these appliances near the cage. When airing the room, the birds should not be subjected to cold draughts or sudden cooling. Sprays of any type can also be very harmful to birds if they are inhaled.

Teaching your budgerigar to 'talk'

Inverted commas have been used to avoid creating the impression that this 'talking' is actually a conscious form of communication. Even if a budgerigar uses some of the words that it has learned in situations where they seem to make sense – some budgerigars will say 'Hello' as soon as the telephone begins to ring – these expressions should not necessarily be interpreted as conscious understanding. There is considerable debate as to whether birds can actually understand what they are repeating.

The importance of trust

A tame budgerigar will soon start making overtures to its owner by holding out its head and fluffing up its feathers slightly. Your bird is expecting to be gently scratched on the side of its head and you should not disappoint it at these moments.

Nearly all birds of the parrot group are expected to have some talent at 'talking'. The budgerigar is among the most talented of 'talkers'.

A relationship of trust is an essential prerequisite for a lesson in talking as the bird should not be distracted by anything else at this time. A further prerequisite is a tender age of 2–3 months as budgerigars will learn to talk much more easily at this age. Finally, as a teacher, you will need a great deal of patience and the good fortune to have found a talented budgerigar. Individual differences with respect to a talent for talking can be quite considerable.

Some budgerigars seem to find talking as easy to learn as flying and are able to pick up a few words or short phrases rapidly. Others tend to mimic sounds from their surroundings, including the calls of garden birds, such as greenfinches or sparrows, which they can hear from the window. Then there are a few budgerigars who will not copy anything and restrict themselves just to their natural means of expression.

A gentle scratch on its head will encourage a budgerigar to become tame.

Lessons

Even at the very beginning of a close relationship with a bird that is still spending a lot of time in a cage, you can keep talking to it in a quiet voice and keep repeating its name. Once it is completely tame and will freely jump onto a proffered finger, you have established the necessary basis of trust and will be able to begin planned lessons. The best time of day is dusk, when you should keep repeating the desired words and phrases. Choose words with sibilants and the vowels 'i' and 'e' because these appear to be particularly easy to imitate. Birds also appear to learn to mimic the voices of women or children more rapidly.

Not immediately, but often after about 2 weeks, you will notice the results of this training. Some budgerigars will even present you with different sounds which were not part of the training and which they have learned by themselves. They are able to add to their repertoire up to about their third year and, in many cases, this may include well over 100 words.

Talking lessons work best if you only have one bird as a pupil. With very great patience you may also achieve a pair of talking birds living together. You will need a very young cock budgerigar and only after he has completed the first stage of his lessons should he be given another extremely young partner. He will look after the newcomer, possibly even feed it during the first few days, and become the young one's teacher.

This effort – and it is a considerable one – should be made by anyone who does not wish to miss the pleasure of having a talkative bird.

Nevertheless, do bear in mind that a budgerigar will probably be happier given the company of another budgerigar rather than just that of its owner.

Should your budgerigar fly free around the room?

Once your budgerigar is tame enough to sit on your hand, you need have no fears and you will be able to leave the cage-door open so that it can fly out. The main thing is that there are no dangers present in the room for your pet.

Naturally, **windows** and **doors** should be closed. This may sound obvious but there are still plenty of people who forget, especially during the hot days of summer. Once a budgerigar has escaped, there is little hope of it returning on its own.

Tame birds may end up in someone else's house – they may even allow themselves to be caught – but the original owner will

almost never get his or her budgerigar back unless it is a good talker and has learned to recite its address and telephone number.

For your birds' first flights around the room, close the **curtains** and cover up all **glass** doors and mirrors. The budgerigar will not know its way around and could fly with full force right into a pane of glass. Concussion or even a broken neck could be the result.

Tall **vases** should be covered. Otherwise, a budgerigar could slide right inside a tall, floor-based vase and die inside, unbeknown to its owner who, meanwhile, is left searching vainly elsewhere for the pet, concluding that it must have escaped.

Further dangers are the **cracks** between large furniture units and walls. Paint containing lead on wallpaper or picture frames has also cost the lives of many adventurous budgerigars as, inevitably, they will start gnawing with their bills. **Hot** cookers, open fires, wood-burning stoves, boilers, cooking pots in the kitchen, poisonous **indoor plants**, **cleaning agents** ... the list is endless and, just as with a small child, you will have to keep watch all the time in order to prevent accidents from happening.

It is a good idea to spend time watching your budgerigar closely during its first flights around the room. The best time to

choose is when you are at home for the weekend.

It will probably be some while before the bird dares to come out of its cage. Naturally, you should refrain from coaxing or forcefully removing the bird from its home. Once it finally dares to venture forth, the first flight will usually finish with the budgerigar perching on a high curtain pelmet or pole. It may remain sitting there for a few hours. Food should only be offered inside the cage, otherwise your pet will not be inclined to return to its home very quickly.

If your budgerigar shows no signs of returning to the cage after this initial flight, leave the bird in peace where it has perched. After dark, close the curtains and, making sure you know exactly where the budgerigar is, turn off the light and you will be able to catch the bird quite easily. Never try to catch your budgerigar by chasing it with a broom and a net. It would take a long time to regain its tameness after such an experience.

Landing on a swing is accomplished with plenty of spirit. It represents a welcome opportunity for some gymnastics.

Breeding

Breeding is a normal part of the life cycle of budgerigars. Even if you have decided to keep a pair of budgerigars, you will have to consider whether you also want a budgerigar nursery.

Whenever you bird is allowed a flying session indoors you should never forget that it is free in the room and may occasionally be walking about on the floor.

Nesting boxes

In the wild, budgerigars generally breed in hollow tree-trunks or holes that have been excavated in trees or branches. Nesting holes may look different and are not always like the classic circular hole made by the woodpecker in a vertical tree-trunk. The breeding place may even be an open, hollow tree-trunk or a horizontal hole in a thick branch.

Fortunately, it is not necessary to provide your budgerigars with a completely natural-looking substitute for a hole or hollow. They will be quite happy with nesting boxes made out of thin plywood, as sold in pet-stores.

Two different types of nesting boxes are generally available: one is **vertical**, with the entry hole in the top half of the front face, and the other is **horizontal**, with the entrance situated to the left or right of the front face. The floor area of the latter is a little larger, which is quite an advantage if there is a large brood of chicks. In addition, the risk of an egg getting broken is reduced because the hen is able to get onto the nest from the side rather than jumping onto it from above – as in the case of the vertical box.

Also it is a lot easier for young birds, when they are ready to fly, to leave the nest if they are reared in a horizontal-style box. They will not need to scrabble up a tall wall to get out. Everything seems to be in favour of this design but the other type continues to be offered for sale.

In contrast to many other birds of the parrot group, hen budgerigars do not like anything on the floor of the nest. If you sprinkle a layer of wood shavings or sawdust on the floor, they will usually scrape it out again.

If you do not mind your pair of budgerigars flying around the room for several weeks, you can even hang the nesting box on the wall like a clock. However, even in this case, on principle the birds should only ever be fed in their cage. If the birds are not allowed to fly around for long periods, then the best plan is to fix the nesting box to the upper half of the side of their cage. In cases where the cage is too small, the only option left is to hang the nesting box in front of the cage door.

Smaller cages will have only one door so

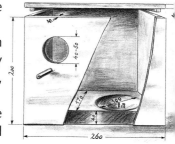

Opposite: Affectionate nibbling – two budgerigars which get on well together.

If you are good at do-it-yourself, making a budgerigar nursery will present no problems. Thin pieces of plywood, softwood or hardboard are suitable materials for the job. Do not forget to make a hollow in the floor for the eggs.

Budgerigars mating.

33

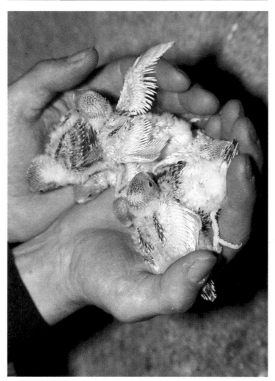

Mating, breeding and rearing.

1. *A nesting box will stimulate the breeding urge of budgerigars.*

2. *The first chicks will hatch from their eggs about 18 days after laying.*

3. *After 8–10 days, the future colouring of the young birds starts to appear on their feathers.*

4. *These three nestlings were hatched at intervals of 3 days, although 3 weeks later you will hardly be able to tell the difference.*

5. *After 4 weeks they will have grown almost all of their feathers.*

the box will have to be taken off daily for feeding and cleaning. Only a particularly tame and patient hen will allow all this to take place without leaving the nest.

Incubation and hatching

Theoretically, budgerigar offspring may be produced at any time of year. The birds are used to taking any favourable opportunity for breeding and it is not limited to a particular time of year. Only when they are moulting and growing new plumage will they refrain from breeding.

Nevertheless, we do not recommend allowing them to breed before early spring. At this time they should be given a nesting box and, in addition to their usual seed mixture, germinated seeds and protein-rich softfood. Despite all these efforts, it will by no means be certain that the pair will begin to breed. As soon as they do start, they should be left undisturbed as far as possible.

Budgerigars are naturally colony-breeders and stimulation from other breeding birds is quite important. It will become quite obvious when they get serious about breeding. The cock will become quite excitable and begin to court his partner. The hen will choose her nesting place or use the nesting box provided.

Eggs are laid at 1-day intervals. With an average of five eggs in the clutch, this means that the first chick to hatch will have grown strong and opened its eyes by the time the fifth chick is just hatching from its egg. In spite of the difference in size, the tiniest one will not generally be neglected. The chicks receive special food from their mother during the first few days of life – a secretion that is formed in the crop.

The breeding hen will only leave the nest for short periods of time, a few times a day, to pass droppings. The quantities of excreta produced are considerable and can be up to a tenth of her body weight.

From the beginning of the breeding period the cock will feed his partner. Once the youngsters have hatched, the hen will still feed at the entrance to the nesting box and will then pass on the food to her young. After about 2 weeks, the cock bird himself will enter the nesting box and feed his offspring directly although he may roost overnight there on a regular basis beforehand.

Care of the chicks

To ensure that the young budgerigars grow into healthy, strong birds, the parents should be provided with good **rearing food** in

36

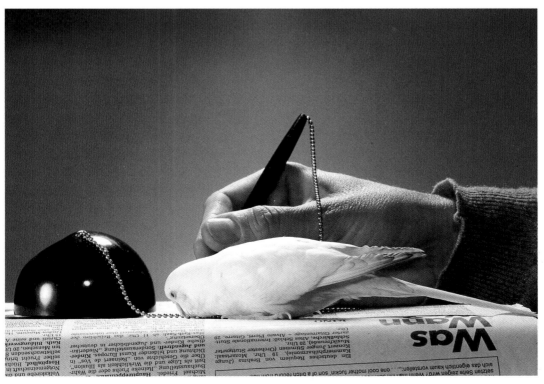

addition to the normal seed. Save time and effort by buying a ready-made rearing-food mixture that can be improved by adding mashed hard-boiled **egg yolk** and finely grated **carrot**. Also recommended is a **vitamin-mineral mixture** in powder form that can be added to their food. Also give them vitamin-rich germinated seeds (see p. 16).

Opposite: You could hardly hope to see a better comparison of the wing feathers of two budgerigars than in this photograph.

Development is as follows:

- The eggs are incubated for 18 days. The young birds remain in the nest for about 5 weeks and then emerge with large black eyes, a blackish bill and slightly washed out markings on their feathers, depending on the colour of their plumage.
- The cock bird then looks after them for another 2 weeks or so, by which time they will be independent.

Usually, the nesting box will be completely dirty by this time and the concave lining the bottom will need to be changed and cleaned thoroughly on a regular basis as the chicks grow older. It should be scrubbed off and allowed to dry thoroughly before being used again. The hen may have laid again by the time that the first clutch of chicks is ready to leave the nest. You should not, however, allow the hen budgerigar to breed more than twice in quick succession as this would be too much for her.

The coloration of budgerigars

In Australia budgerigars in the wild are mainly green. Very rarely you may see an occasional yellow one in a large flock but their survival rate is fairly low because, without the camouflaging green colour, they soon fall victim to predatory birds.

Strictly speaking, green is not a true colour because it is made up of two components. Most people have mixed colours in a paintbox when they were children and know that blue and yellow mixed together produce green. A similar thing happens naturally, except that the whole matter is a little more complicated than on a palette.

How colours are mixed naturally

To explain it simply, there are two pigments in budgerigars: a yellow pigment in the plumage and a dark melanin pigment beneath the so-called 'blue layer'. The colour of a budgerigar is due to the presence or absence, and the distribution, of one or both of these pigments. If the yellow pigment is missing,

The topography of a budgerigar:

1. Cere
2. Upper bill
3. Cheek patch
4. Throat spots
5. Breast
6. Belly
7. Upper leg
8. Tarsus
9. Tail feathers
10. Primaries
11. Secondaries
12. Back
13. Alula

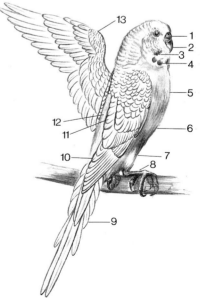

A typical picture: Budgerigars occupied with feeding each other.

the bird will appear **blue** as a result of light passing through the blue layer and reflecting off the melanin layer. If the melanin pigment is missing, the bird will be **yellow**. If both pigments are missing, the bird will be **white**, although a faint bluish tinge may be visible in some lights because the blue layer is still present. In **green** budgerigars melanin is present in the central areas of the feathers while the yellow pigment is present in the outer layers.

All the many shades of colour and the multi-coloured budgerigars can be explained by this simple basic rule. The colours will never leave the range of blue – yellow – green – white. Red is not possible and will never occur, no matter how much some ambitious breeder might dream about it, although black may possibly be achieved in the future.

To most budgerigars it does not seem to matter at all what colour partner they have. However, how budgerigars are paired is important to anyone hoping to produce particular colours as a result of a breeding programme.

Shades of colours and other mutations

As can be seen in many examples, both naturally occurring and from artificial breeding, certain variations affecting both plumage and markings will inevitably appear. The first mutation recorded in budgerigars was a yellow variant produced in Belgium in 1872.

Changes in the budgerigar's pattern of markings have also occurred, giving rise to the **opaline** variety, in which the barring on the head is less prominent. Changes to the black markings on the head and on the wings have produced the **cinnamon** budgerigars, as well as other colours, such as **grey-wings**.

There have also been other kinds of mutation that have affected the shape of the feathers, e.g. the **crested** budgerigars, in which the feathers grow in all directions and form an almost regular crest along the head. Not all mutations are welcome, however, e.g. the so-called '**feather-dusters**' with abnormally long feathers. Such birds tend to have a shortened life-span and are not deliberately bred, although they do crop up on occasions.

Opposite: This white budgerigar is visibly at home with its new friend and playmate.

Coloration and colour combinations of budgerigars:

1. *The colours of budgerigars can be divided into two main groups: green and blue. The green forms include light green, dark green, olive-green, grey-green and yellow. Among the blue forms are light blue, dark blue, mauve, violet, grey and white.*

2. *The albino bird is white all over and has red eyes.*

3. *This light green bird represents the wild form of budgerigar.*

4. *In a yellow budgerigar, the dark melanin pigment that would otherwise combine with the yellow pigment to form a rich green colour is absent.*

5. *A so-called 'grey' budgerigar displays an even grey colour on its underside and back.*

6. *Blue series budgerigars usually have white facial coloration although a yellow-faced mutation does exist and can be combined with any of the blue shades.*